Stories for the Romantic Heart

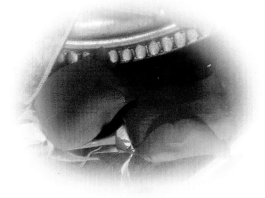

COMPILED by ALICE GRAY

MULTNOMAH GIFTS™

Multnomah® Publishers Sisters, Oregon

Stories for the Romantic Heart

©2002 by Multnomah Publishers, Inc.
published by Multnomah Publishers, Inc.
P.O. Box 1720, Sisters, Oregon 97759

ISBN 1-57673-919-8

Designed by Koechel Peterson & Associates, Minneapolis, Minnesota

Multnomah Publishers, Inc., has made every effort to trace
the ownership of all poems and quotes.
In the event of a question arising from the use of a poem or quote,
we regret any error made and will be pleased to make
the necessary correction in future editions of this book.

Please see the acknowledgments at the back of the book
for complete attributions for this material.

Scripture quotations are taken from *The Holy Bible*, New International Version
©1973, 1984 by International Bible Society, used by permission of
Zondervan Publishing House.

Multnomah is a trademark of Multnomah Publishers, Inc.,
and is registered in the U.S. Patent and Trademark Office.
The colophon is a trademark of Multnomah Publishers, Inc.

Printed in China

02 03 04 05 06 07 08—10 9 8 7 6 5 4 3 2 1 0

www.multnomahgifts.com

TABLE OF CONTENTS

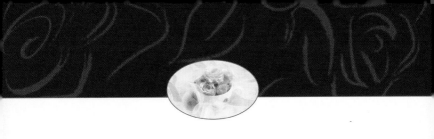

A Gentle Caress

DAPHNA RENAN

*M*ichael and I hardly noticed when the waitress came and placed the plates on our table. We were seated in a small deli tucked away from the bustle of Third Street in New York City. Even the smell of our recently arrived blintzes was no challenge to our excited chatter. In fact, the blintzes remained slumped in their sour cream for quite some time. We were enjoying ourselves too much to eat.

Our exchange was lively, if not profound. We laughed about the movie that we had seen the night before and disagreed about the meaning behind the text we had just finished for our literature seminar. He told me about the moment he had taken a drastic step into maturity by becoming Michael and refusing to respond to "Mikey." Had he been twelve or fourteen? He couldn't remember,

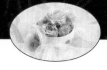

but he did recall that his mother had cried and said he was growing up too quickly. As we finally bit into our blueberry blintzes, I told him about the blueberries that my sister and I used to pick when we went to visit our cousins in the country. I recalled that I always finished mine before we got back to the house, and my aunt would warn me that I was going to get a bad stomachache. Of course, I never did.

As our sweet conversation continued, my eyes glanced across the restaurant, stopping at the small corner booth where an elderly couple sat. The woman's floral-print dress seemed as faded as the cushion on which she had rested her worn handbag. The top of the man's head was as shiny as the soft-boiled egg he slowly nibbled. She also ate her oatmeal at a slow, almost tedious, pace.

But what drew my thoughts to them was their undisturbed silence. It seemed to me that a melancholy emptiness permeated their little corner. As the exchange between Michael and me fluctuated from laughs to

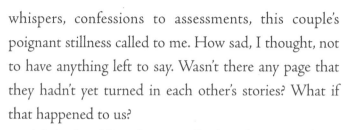

whispers, confessions to assessments, this couple's poignant stillness called to me. How sad, I thought, not to have anything left to say. Wasn't there any page that they hadn't yet turned in each other's stories? What if that happened to us?

Michael and I paid our small tab and got up to leave the restaurant. As we walked by the corner where the old couple sat, I accidentally dropped my wallet. Bending over to pick it up, I noticed that under the table, each of their free hands was gently cradled in the other's. They had been holding hands all this time!

I stood up feeling humbled by the simple yet profound act of connection I had just been privileged to witness. This man's gentle caress of his wife's tired fingers filled not only what I had previously perceived as an emotionally empty corner, but also my heart. Theirs was not the uncomfortable silence that threatens to fill the space after the punch line or at the end of an anecdote on a first date. No, theirs was a comfortable, relaxed ease, a gentle

love that did not always need words to express itself. They had probably shared this hour of the morning with each other for a long time, and maybe today wasn't that different from yesterday, but they were at peace with that—and with each other.

Maybe, I thought as Michael and I walked out, it wouldn't be so bad if someday that were us. Maybe it would be kind of nice.

Great love, through smallest channels,

will find its surest way;

It waits not state occasions,

which may not come, or may,

It comforts and it blesses,

hour by hour and day by day.

AUTHOR UNKNOWN

Do You Remember Me?

ARNOLD FINE

As I walked home one freezing day, I stumbled on a wallet someone had lost in the street. I picked it up and looked inside to find some identification so I could call the owner. But the wallet contained only three dollars and a crumpled letter that looked as though it had been in there for years.

The envelope was worn and the only thing that was legible on it was the return address. I started to open the letter, hoping to find some clue. Then I saw the date—1924. The letter had been written almost sixty years ago.

It was written in a beautiful feminine handwriting on powder blue stationery with a little flower in the left-hand corner. It was a "Dear John" letter that told the recipient, whose name appeared to be Michael, that the writer could

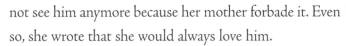

not see him anymore because her mother forbade it. Even so, she wrote that she would always love him.

It was signed Hannah.

It was a beautiful letter, but there was no way except for the name Michael, that the owner could be identified. Maybe if I called information the operator could find a phone listing for the address on the envelope.

"Operator," I began, "this is an unusual request. I'm trying to find the owner of a wallet that I found. Is there

any way you can tell me if there is a phone number for an address that was on an envelope in the wallet?"

She suggested I speak with her supervisor, who hesitated for a moment then said, "Well, there is a phone listing at that address, but I can't give you the number." She said, as a courtesy, she would call that number, explain my story and would ask them if they wanted her to connect me. I waited a few minutes and then she was back on the line. "I have a party who will speak with you."

I asked the woman on the other end of the line if she knew anyone by the name of Hannah. She gasped, "Oh! We bought this house from a family who had a daughter named Hannah. But that was thirty years ago!"

"Would you know where that family could be located now?" I asked.

"I remember that Hannah had to place her mother in a nursing home some years ago," the woman said. "Maybe if you got in touch with them they might be able to track down the daughter."

She gave me the name of the nursing home and I called the number. They told me the old lady had passed away some years ago but they did have a phone number for where they thought the daughter might be living.

I thanked them and phoned. The woman who answered explained that Hannah herself was now living in a nursing home.

This whole thing was stupid, I thought to myself. Why was I making such a big deal over finding the owner of a wallet that had only three dollars and a letter that was almost sixty years old?

Nevertheless, I called the nursing home in which Hannah was supposed to be living and the man who answered the phone told me, "Yes, Hannah is staying with us."

Even though it was already 10 p.m., I asked if I could come by to see her. "Well," he said hesitatingly, "if you want to take a chance, she might be in the day room watching television."

I thanked him and drove over to the nursing home.

The night nurse and a guard greeted me at the door. We went up to the third floor of the large building. In the day room, the nurse introduced me to Hannah.

She was a sweet, silver-haired old-timer with a warm smile and a twinkle in her eye. I told her about finding the wallet and showed her the letter. The second she saw the powder blue envelope with that little flower on the left, she took a deep breath and said, "Young man, this letter was the last contact I ever had with Michael."

She looked away for a moment deep in thought and then said softly, "I loved him very much. But I was only sixteen at the time and my mother felt I was too young. Oh, he was so handsome. He looked like Sean Connery, the actor."

"Yes," she continued. "Michael Goldstein was a wonderful person. If you should find him, tell him I think of him often. And," she hesitated for a moment, almost biting her lip, "tell him I still love him. You know," she said smiling as tears began to well up in her eyes, "I never did marry. I guess no one ever matched up to Michael...."

I thanked Hannah and said good-bye. I took the elevator to the first floor and as I stood by the door, the guard there asked, "Was the old lady able to help you?"

I told him she had given me a lead. "At least I have a name, but I think I'll let it go for a while. I spent almost the whole day trying to find the owner of this wallet."

I had taken out the wallet, which was a simple brown leather case with red lacing on the side. When the guard saw it, he said, "Hey, wait a minute! That's Mr. Goldstein's wallet. I'd know it anywhere with that bright red lacing. He's always losing that wallet. I must have found it in the hall at least three times."

"Who's Mr. Goldstein?" I asked as my hand began to shake.

"He's one of the old-timers on the eighth floor. That's Mike Goldstein's wallet for sure. He must have lost it on one of his walks."

I thanked the guard and quickly ran back to the nurse's office. I told her what the guard had said. We went back

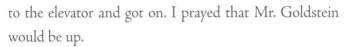

to the elevator and got on. I prayed that Mr. Goldstein would be up.

On the eighth floor, the floor nurse said, "I think he's still in the day room. He likes to read at night. He's a darling old man."

We went to the only room that had any lights on and there was a man reading a book. The nurse went over to him and asked if he had lost his wallet. Mr. Goldstein looked up with surprise, put his hand in his back pocket and said, "Oh, it is missing!"

"This kind gentleman found a wallet and we wondered if it could be yours?"

I handed Mr. Goldstein the wallet and the second he saw it, he smiled with relief and said, "Yes, that's it! It must have dropped out of my pocket this afternoon. I want to give you a reward."

"No, thank you," I said. "But I have to tell you something. I read the letter in the hope of finding out who owned the wallet."

The smile on his face suddenly disappeared. "You read that letter?"

"Not only did I read it, I think I know where Hannah is."

He suddenly grew pale. "Hannah? You know where she is? How is she? Is she still as pretty as she was? Please, please tell me," he begged.

"She's fine...just as pretty as when you knew her," I said softly.

The old man smiled with anticipation and asked,

"Could you tell me where she is? I want to call her tomorrow." He grabbed my hand and said, "You know something, mister, I was so in love with that girl that when that letter came, my life literally ended. I never married. I guess I've always loved her."

"Mr. Goldstein," I said. "Come with me."

We took the elevator down to the third floor. The hallways were darkened and only one or two little nightlights lit our way to the day room where Hannah was sitting alone watching the television. The nurse walked over to her.

"Hannah," she said softly, pointing to Michael, who was waiting with me in the doorway. "Do you know this man?"

She adjusted her glasses, looked for a moment, but didn't say a word. Michael said softly, almost in a whisper, "Hannah, it's Michael. Do you remember me?"

She gasped, "Michael! I don't believe it! Michael! It's you! My Michael!" He walked slowly toward her and they embraced. The nurse and I left with tears streaming down our faces.

"See," I said. "See how the good Lord works. If it's meant to be, it will be."

About three weeks later I got a call at my office from the nursing home. "Can you break away on Sunday to attend a wedding? Michael and Hannah are going to be married!"

It was a beautiful wedding with all the people at the nursing home dressed up to join in the celebration. Hannah wore a light beige dress and looked beautiful. Michael wore a dark blue suit and stood tall. They made me their best man.

The hospital gave them their own room and if you ever wanted to see a seventy-six-year-old bride and a seventy-nine-year-old groom acting like two teenagers, you had to see this couple.

A perfect ending for a love affair that lasted nearly sixty years.

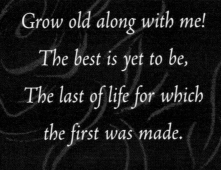

Grow old along with me!
The best is yet to be,
The last of life for which
the first was made.

ROBERT BROWNING

Somewhere there waiteth in this world of ours

For one lone soul another lonely soul,

Each choosing each through all the weary hours,

And meeting strangely at one sudden goal,

Then blend they, like green leaves

with golden flowers,

Into one beautiful and perfect whole;

And life's long night is ended, and the way

Lies open onward to eternal day.

EDWIN ARNOLD

The Mystery of Marriage

MIKE MASON

The first thing I see, as I open my eyes, is the morning making a pink glow on the trunks of the three birch trees outside our window. Between two of the trunks hangs the moon, just past full and sinking in the west, the same pale, chalky-pink color as the papery bark of the birches. Both trees and moon appear almost translucent, as if lit from behind.

But the whole morning is translucent. The air holds light like a goblet. Even the mountain, that most opaque of God's creations, glows with an inner light....

This is the scene I wake up to every morning, here where I live, to the accompaniment of one of those frothing, silver-blue, rushing mountain rivers whose sound fills my ears the way the dawn light fills my eyes. And yet even that is not all. There is something else. Something more breathtaking than any of these other stupendous and beautiful things, and even more radiant with light.

My wife is lying in bed beside me. Right this moment I could reach out my hand and touch her, as easily as I touch myself, and as I think about this, it is more staggering than any mountain or moon. It is even more staggering, I think, than if this woman happened instead to be an angel (which, come to think of it, she might well be). There are only two factors which prevent this situation from being so overpoweringly awesome that my heart would explode just trying to take it in: one is that I have woken up just like this, with the same woman beside me, hundreds of times before; and the other is that millions of other men and women are waking up beside each other, just like this, each and every day all around the world, and have been for thousands of years.

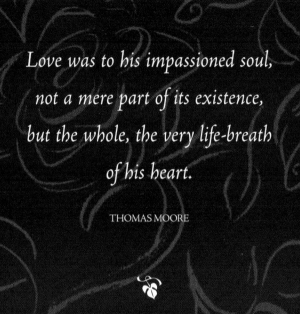

Love was to his impassioned soul,

not a mere part of its existence,

but the whole, the very life-breath

of his heart.

THOMAS MOORE

Love in a Locket

GEERY HOWE

As a seminar leader, I hear a lot of stories about people's lives and experiences. One day at the end of a seminar, a woman came up to me and told me about an event that changed her life—and in the telling, touched mine.

used to think I was just a nurse," she began, "until one day a couple of years ago.

"It was noontime and I was feeding 'the feeders,' the elderly who cannot feed themselves. Messy work, keeping track of each one and making sure they keep the food in their mouths. I looked up as an elderly gentleman passed by the dining room doorway. He was on his way down the hall for a daily visit with his wife.

"Our eyes met over the distance, and I knew right then in my heart that I should be with them both that noon hour. My coworker covered for me, and I followed him down the corridor.

"When I entered the room, she was lying in bed, looking up at the ceiling with her arms across her chest. He was sitting in the chair at the end of the bed with his arms crossed, looking at the floor.

"I walked over to her and said, 'Susan, is there anything you want to share today? If so, I came down to lis-

ten.' She tried to speak but her lips were dry and nothing came out. I bent over closer and asked again.

"'Susan, if you cannot say it with words, can you show me with your hands?'

"She carefully lifted her hands off her chest and held them up before her eyes. They were old hands, with leathery skin and swollen knuckles, worn from years of caring, working, and living. She then grasped the collar of her nightgown and began to pull.

"I unbuttoned the top buttons. She reached in and pulled out a long gold chain connected to a small gold locket. She held it up, and tears came to her eyes.

"Her husband got up from the end of the bed and came over. Sitting beside her, he took his hands and tenderly placed them around hers. 'There is a story about this locket,' he explained, and he began to tell it to me.

"'One day many months ago, we awoke early and I told Susan I could no longer care for her by myself. I could not carry her to the bathroom, keep the house clean, plus cook all the meals. My body could no longer do this. I, too, had aged.

"'We talked long and hard that morning. She told me to go to coffee club and ask where a good place might be. I didn't return until lunchtime. We chose here from the advice of others.

"'On the first day, after all the forms, the weighing and the tests, the nurse told us that her fingers were so swollen that they would need to cut off the wedding rings.

"'After everyone left the room, we sat together and she asked me, 'What do we do with a broken ring and a whole ring?' For I had chosen to take off my ring that day, too.

"'Both of these rings were old, more oval than round. Thin in some places and strong in other parts. We made a difficult decision. That was the hardest night in my entire life. It was the first time we had slept apart in forty-three years.

"'The next morning I took the two rings to the jewelers and had them melted. Half of that locket is my ring, and the other half is hers. The clasp is made from the engagement ring that I gave her when I proposed to her, down by the pond at the back of the farm on a warm summer's evening. She told me it was about time and answered yes.

"'On the inside it says *I love you, Susan* and on the other side it says *I love you, Joseph.* We made this locket because we were afraid that one day we might not be able to say these words to each other.'

"He picked her up and held her gently in his arms. I knew that I was the channel, and they had the message. I slipped out the door and went back to feeding the feeders with more kindness in my heart.

"After lunch and the paperwork, I walked back down to their room. He was rocking her in his arms and singing the last verse of 'Amazing Grace.' I waited while he laid her down, crossed her arms and closed her eyes.

"He turned to me at the door and said, 'Thank you. She passed away just a little bit ago. Thank you very much.'

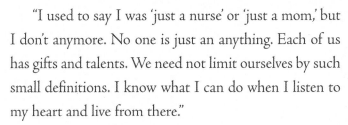

"I used to say I was 'just a nurse' or 'just a mom,' but I don't anymore. No one is just an anything. Each of us has gifts and talents. We need not limit ourselves by such small definitions. I know what I can do when I listen to my heart and live from there."

As she finished her story, we hugged and she left. I stood in the doorway with thankfulness.

Henceforth there will be such a oneness between us—
that when one weeps the other will taste salt.

AUTHOR UNKNOWN

True love's the gift
which God hath given,
To man alone beneath the heaven.
The silver link, the silver tie,
Which heart to heart,
and mind to mind,
In body and in soul can bind.

SIR WALTER SCOTT

With This Ring

RUTH BELL GRAHAM

"With this ring..."
your strong, familiar voice
fell like a benediction
on my heart, that dusk;
tall candles flickered gently,
our age-old vows were said,
and I could hear
someone begin to sing
an old, old song,
timeworn and lovely,
timeworn and dear.
And in that dusk
were old, old friends—
and you,
an old friend, too
(and dearer than them all).

More Beautiful

AUTHOR UNKNOWN

The question is asked, "Is there anything more beautiful in life than a boy and girl clasping clean hands and pure hearts in the path of marriage? Can there be anything more beautiful than young love?"

And the answer is given. "Yes, there is a more beautiful thing. It is the spectacle of an old man and an old woman finishing their journey together on that path. Their hands are gnarled, but still clasped; their faces are seamed, but still radiant; their hearts are physically bowed and tired, but still strong with love and devotion for one another. Yes, there is a more beautiful thing than young love. Old love."

Young love is a flame;

very pretty,

often very hot and fierce,

but still only light and flickering.

The love of the older

and disciplined heart

is as coals,

deep-burning,

unquenchable.

HENRY WARD BEECHER

House on the Lake

MIKE ROYKO

*W*hen the two of them started spending weekends at the quiet Wisconsin lake, they were young and had little money. Her relatives let them use a tiny cottage in the wooded hollow a mile or so from the water.

He worked odd hours, so often they wouldn't get there until after midnight on a Friday. But if the mosquitoes weren't out, they'd go for a moonlight swim, then rest with their backs against a tree and sip wine and talk about their future.

One summer the young man bought an old motorboat. They'd ride along the shoreline, looking at the houses and wondering what it would be like to have a place on the water. He'd just shake his head; those houses cost more than he could ever afford.

Years passed. They had kids, and they didn't go to the little cottage as often. Finally her relatives sold the place.

Then he got lucky in his work, making more money than he ever dreamed they'd have. Remembering those weekends, they went back and bought a home on the water. A cedar house surrounded by big old trees, where the land sloped gently down to the shore. It was perfect.

They hadn't known summers could be that good. In the mornings he'd go fishing before it was light. She'd sleep until the birds woke her. Then he'd make breakfast, and they'd eat omelettes on the deck.

They got to know the chipmunks, the squirrels, and a woodpecker who took over their biggest tree. They got to know the grocer, the butcher who smoked his own bacon, the farmer who sold them vine-ripened tomatoes.

The best part of their day was dusk. She loved sunsets. They'd always stop to watch the sun go down, changing the color of the lake from blue, to purple, to silver, and then to black. One evening he made up a small poem:

The sun rolls down
Like a golden tear
Another day,
Another day
Gone.

She told him that it was sad, but that she liked it.

What she didn't like was October, even with its beautiful colors and evenings spent in front of the fireplace. She was a summer person. The cold wind wasn't her friend.

In November they would store the boat, take down the hammock, lock everything tight and drive back to the city. She'd always sigh as they left.

Finally spring would come, and when they knew the ice on the lake was gone, they'd be back. She'd throw open the doors and windows and let in the fresh air. Then she'd go out and greet the chipmunks and the woodpeckers.

Every summer seemed better than the last. The sunsets seemed more spectacular. And more precious.

Then one weekend he went alone to close the place down for the winter.

He worked quickly, trying not to let himself think that this particular chair had been her favorite, that the hammock had been her Christmas gift to him, that the house on the lake had been his gift to her.

He didn't work quickly enough. He was still there at sunset. It was a great burst of orange, the kind she had loved best.

He tried, but he couldn't watch it alone. Not through tears. So he turned his back on it, went inside, drew the draperies, locked the door, and drove away.

Later there would be a For Sale sign out front. Maybe a couple that loved to quietly watch sunsets together would like it. He hoped so.

The heart…like the sun in its course,
sees nothing, from the dewdrop
to the ocean, but a mirror
which it brightens,
and warms, and fills.

JEAN PAUL RICHTER

The Table

JOHN V. A. WEAVER

*N*o, it isn't much of a table to look at. Just on old yellow oak thing, I suppose you'd call it. It isn't that we couldn't have had mahogany or walnut, of course. Only—well, thirty-eight years sort of turns anything into a treasure.

It was Sam's father's wedding present to us. It and the six chairs—four plain-bottomed, two with leather seats.

I recollect as well as yesterday the first supper we ate at it. We came back from our honeymoon in Canada on a Monday afternoon. Sam had made the lease for the little five-room house on Locust Street the week before we got married.

All the month we were up there lazying around and fishing and getting used to each other I was worried about what we were going to do for furnishing the dining room. I had a good deal of furniture from Mother's house, and Sam had some from his flat, but neither of us had a dining room table. We had talked a lot about it. But that trouble was settled the minute we went into the room and saw the yellow oak, bright and shiny, with a note from Father Graham on it.

I scrambled around and got some sort of a meal together. What it was doesn't matter.

Pretty soon we were sitting in the chairs opposite each other, so close we could touch hands.

Sam didn't pay much attention to the food.

He kept looking at me. You know the way newlyweds will go on. Sam didn't say anything for a minute. Then he looked at me, and said, "I guess you're about the prettiest girl anywhere, Mary. I'm glad this table is so short. It lets me see you all the better."

I had to laugh. "Why, silly," I answered, "it opens in the middle. There's extra leaves in the china closet. We can make it as long as we want!"

He looked a little sheepish, and glanced around at the four other chairs. Then he grinned.

"Well," he said, "we'll have to use those leaves before we get through, I reckon."

I couldn't half eat for laughing. Yes, and blushing, too.

See that whole row of round dents up next to my place? That's what Sallie did with her spoon. She was the only one that always hammered. She was the first.

Over there, right by the opening—that's where Sam Jr. tried to carve his initials one time when he was about five. Sam caught him just as he was finishing the "S." It was a warm night for one young man, I can tell you.

Of course we'd put in one of the extra leaves a good many times before Ben came. The children were forever having friends over. Ben made the extra leaf permanent.

Then we commenced adding the second leaf. More friends, you see. Sam kept moving farther away from me, I used to tell him. He'd always answer the same thing. "My eyesight's all right," he'd say. "I can see just as well

how pretty you are." And he said it as if he meant it.

So the children grew up and the table came to its longest. Sallie married Tom Thorpe when she was nineteen, and they both lived with us for three years.

The boys were in high school then, and I tell you we made a big family. All three extra leaves hardly did. Sam at one end and me at the other, Ben and Sam Jr. and Sallie and Tom—and my first granddaughter, Irene, in her high chair.

But she had her place, too. By that time we were in the big house on Maple, and the noise—and the life—and the happiness! The table was certainly getting battle-scarred. Look at that brown burnt place. That's where Senator Berkeley put down his cigar the night he stopped with us.

Well, then, Sam Jr. went off to college, and a little while after that Tom and Sallie set up housekeeping in their own home up on the Heights. So one of the leaves came out for good, and we didn't have so much use for the second, except for company once in a while. Except vacations, of course.

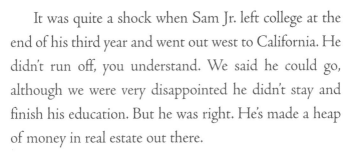

It was quite a shock when Sam Jr. left college at the end of his third year and went out west to California. He didn't run off, you understand. We said he could go, although we were very disappointed he didn't stay and finish his education. But he was right. He's made a heap of money in real estate out there.

He comes back once a year for a week or so with Myra, that's his wife, and their two youngsters. Then the old table gets swollen back to its biggest. It seems mighty quiet when they go.

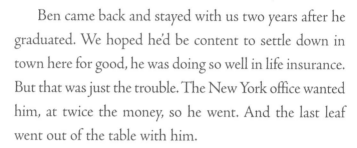

Ben came back and stayed with us two years after he graduated. We hoped he'd be content to settle down in town here for good, he was doing so well in life insurance. But that was just the trouble. The New York office wanted him, at twice the money, so he went. And the last leaf went out of the table with him.

That's been a year now. Sometimes I think of taking a roomer. Not just any ragtag and bobtail; some nice young fellow who needs a good home. It's so quiet.

I said so to Sam the other night. "My goodness," I said, "the table's so little again. Why, you're right on top of me. You can see all my wrinkles."

Sam laughed, and then he put his hand out and squeezed mine. "My eyes have grown dim to correspond," he answered. "You look as beautiful to me as ever. I guess you're about the prettiest girl anywhere."

But, still....

56

Time flies,

Suns rise,

And shadows fall.

Let time go by.

Love is forever over all.

AUTHOR UNKNOWN

Love Shines Through

AUTHOR UNKNOWN

The passengers on the bus watched sympathetically as the attractive young woman with the white cane made her way carefully up the steps. She paid the driver and, using her hands to feel the location of the seats, walked down the aisle and found a seat he'd told her was

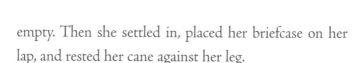

empty. Then she settled in, placed her briefcase on her lap, and rested her cane against her leg.

It had been a year since Susan, thirty-four, became blind. Due to a medical misdiagnosis she had been rendered sightless, and she was suddenly thrown into a world of darkness, anger, frustration, and self-pity. Once a fiercely independent woman, Susan now felt condemned by this terrible twist of fate to become a powerless, helpless burden on everyone around her. "How could this have happened to me?" she would plead, her heart knotted with anger.

But no matter how much she cried or ranted or prayed, she knew the painful truth—her sight was never going to return. A cloud of depression hung over Susan's once optimistic spirit. Just getting through each day was an exercise in frustration and exhaustion. And all she had to cling to was her husband, Mark.

Mark was an air force officer and he loved Susan with all of his heart. When she first lost her sight, he watched her sink into despair and was determined to help his wife

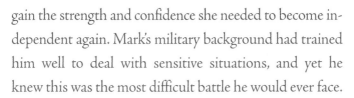

gain the strength and confidence she needed to become independent again. Mark's military background had trained him well to deal with sensitive situations, and yet he knew this was the most difficult battle he would ever face.

Finally, Susan felt ready to return to her job, but how would she get there? She used to take the bus, but was now too frightened to get around the city by herself. Mark volunteered to drive her to work each day, even though they worked at opposite ends of the city.

At first, this comforted Susan and fulfilled Mark's need to protect his sightless wife who was so insecure about performing the slightest task. Soon, however, Mark realized that this arrangement wasn't working—it was hectic and costly. *Susan is going to have to start taking the bus again,* he admitted to himself. But just the thought of mentioning it to her made him cringe. She was still so fragile, so angry. How would she react?

Just as Mark predicted, Susan was horrified at the idea of taking the bus again. "I'm blind!" she responded

bitterly. "How am I supposed to know where I'm going? I feel like you're abandoning me."

Mark's heart broke to hear these words, but he knew what had to be done. He promised Susan that each morning and evening he would ride the bus with her, for as long as it took, until she got the hang of it. And that is exactly what happened.

For two solid weeks, Mark, military uniform and all, accompanied Susan to and from work each day. He taught her how to rely on her other senses, specifically her hearing, to determine where she was and how to adapt to her new environment. He helped her befriend the bus drivers who could watch out for her and save her a seat. He made her laugh, even on those not-so-good days when she would trip exiting the bus, or drop her briefcase.

Each morning they made the journey together, and Mark would take a cab back to his office. Although this routine was even more costly and exhausting than the previous one, Mark knew it was only a matter of time before Susan would be able to ride the bus on her own. He believed in her, in the Susan he used to know before she'd lost her sight, who wasn't afraid of any challenge and who would never, ever quit.

Finally, Susan decided that she was ready to try the trip on her own. Monday morning arrived, and before she left, she threw her arms around Mark, her temporary bus riding companion, her husband, and her best friend.

Her eyes filled with tears of gratitude for his loyalty, his patience, his love. She said good-bye, and for the first time, they went their separate ways. Monday, Tuesday, Wednesday, Thursday.... Each day on her own went perfectly, and Susan had never felt better. She was doing it! She was going to work all by herself!

On Friday morning, Susan took the bus to work as usual. As she was paying for her fare to exit the bus, the driver said, "Boy, I sure envy you." Susan wasn't certain if the driver was speaking to her or not. After all, who on earth would ever envy a blind woman who had struggled just to find the courage to live for the past year?

Curious, she asked the driver, "Why do you say that you envy me?"

The driver responded, "It must feel so good to be taken care of and protected like you are."

Susan had no idea what the driver was talking about and asked again, "What do you mean?"

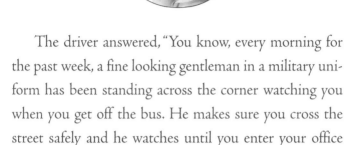

The driver answered, "You know, every morning for the past week, a fine looking gentleman in a military uniform has been standing across the corner watching you when you get off the bus. He makes sure you cross the street safely and he watches until you enter your office building. Then he blows you a kiss, gives you a little salute, and walks away. You are one lucky lady."

Tears of happiness poured down Susan's cheeks. For although she couldn't physically see him, she had always felt Mark's presence. She was lucky, so lucky, for he had given her a gift more powerful than sight, a gift she didn't need to see to believe—the gift of love that can bring light where there had been darkness.

Love never asks how much must I do,
but how much can I do.

FREDERICK A. AGAR

Grandmother's Secret

AUTHOR UNKNOWN

*E*ven the most devoted couple will experience a storm once in a while. A grandmother, celebrating her golden wedding anniversary, once told the secret of her long and happy marriage.

"On my wedding day I decided to make a list of ten of my husband's faults which for the sake of our marriage, I would overlook," she said. "I never did get around to listing them. But whenever my husband did something I didn't like, I would say to myself, 'Lucky for him that's one of the ten.'"

He who covers over an offense promotes love.

PROVERBS 17:9

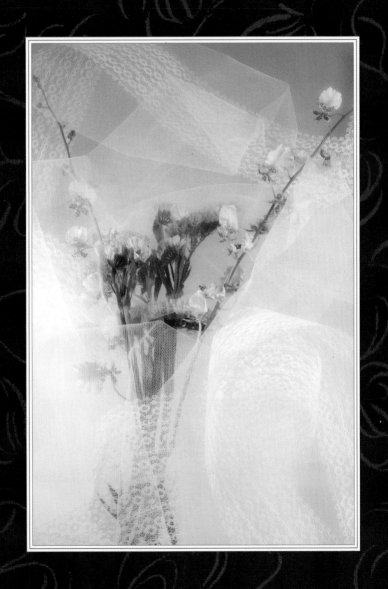

Love's ABCs

AUTHOR UNKNOWN

Love

Accepts, Behaves, Cheers, Defends,
Enriches, Forgives, Grows, and Helps.

Love

Includes, Joins, Kneels, Listens,
Motivates, Notices, Overlooks,
and Provides.

Love

Quiets, Respects, Surprises, Tries,
Understands, Volunteers, Warms,
Xpects, and Yields.
Love in action adds Zip to your life.

Levi's Valentine

J. STEPHEN LANG

When Levi Carpenter proposed to Letitia (Letty) McCluskey on New Year's Eve 1919, he said, "Pick a day [for our wedding], and make it one I can always remember."

She chose February 14.

That year, 1920, a foot of snow fell in Fayetteville, Tennessee, on Valentine's Day. Letty said, "Let's put it off a week, to make sure all the guests can arrive." Levi wouldn't hear of it. He was convinced the day was right, snow or no snow. The wedding was hastily moved from the church to the minister's parlor, with five people present.

Because the roads were impassable, all arrangements for flowers, refreshments, and formal wear had been scrapped. Yet, as if by magic, Levi arrived with a bouquet of pink roses for his bride. When prodded, he said he "had connections." Forty-some years later, he confided to me (his great-grandson) that the minister's wife brought them from her own greenhouse.

By the time I came into the world, Levi and his Valentine wife were well past sixty. Living only a few miles away, I saw them almost every weekend. After Valentine's Day, without fail, I knew a huge bouquet of pink roses would be on the mahogany table in the foyer. But that wasn't all.

Somewhere near the vase was Levi's one annual attempt at artistry: a large snowflake intricately cut from paper. Attached to it was a note: "To Letty, my Valentine lady these 44 years." The words never changed from year to year, just the number. Yet true to nature, the snowflakes were always a different design.

At age nine, I discovered a nook in the china cabinet where every anniversary snowflake had been placed, lovingly and dearly, starting with the first one inscribed, "To Letty, my Valentine for a whole year." Levi, a carpenter who was considered "tight-lipped" and unemotional, showed his heart to everyone once a year.

One day Levi sat me down and patiently showed me, step-by-step, how to fold and cut paper snowflakes. But it didn't take long before I became more frustrated than artistic. My efforts resulted in things that looked more like rat's nests than snowflakes. It made me wonder: Does Great-Granddad really want me to know the secret?

He seemed to delight in being the only one in the family with an artistic gift. He knew his wealthy brother Claude had taken his wife on a Valentine jaunt to the Caribbean, giving her a pearl necklace on the way. But Claude could only buy gifts. Levi could make snowflakes. And every one was a reminder of his wedding day, and of the girl he married.

No one ever said to me on February 14, "This is a big day for your great-grandparents." But I knew it was. The only time I recall them kissing was on a Valentine's Day, when my parents and I just happened to arrive at the moment Levi gave Letty her annual snowflake and roses.

When she realized we were watching, Letty's cheeks flushed as she scurried from the room, shrieking, "Levi, you wicked thing!" She wasn't convincing at all.

A few years afterward Levi gave Letty a snowflake on which he had written, "To Letty, my Valentine lady these 56 years." No one was sure if Letty saw this one. She was alive, and conscious, but so heavily medicated that she could only nod faintly when Levi held the snowflake in front of her. He placed it on her bedside table in the nursing home, beside the vase of pink roses.

He turned to Letty and said, "I'll be in tomorrow, early, Letty." Then after a pause, he added, "my love." She nodded faintly again.

Levi took my arm—a rare occurrence—as we left the room. A few feet down the corridor he said, "Boy, go get that snowflake. Them nurses or cleanin' women may throw it out with the garbage."

I retrieved it, knowing Levi intended to take it home

to the china cabinet with the others. If Letty ever came home, he would show it to her then.

The following Valentine's Day, Levi and I made our way to the cemetery, bringing a bouquet of pink roses. There was a light dusting of snow, and he brushed it away from the double headstone. He placed the roses in the headstone's vase, hesitated, then put them back in the glass vase he'd brought them in.

"This is foolish, boy," he said. "No point in leavin' these here where no one'll see them."

He let out a deep breath, then said, "She'll see 'em, anyway, wherever they are. We'll come back in April. I'm thinkin' of plantin' a rose bush here, if the church won't mind."

"Pink roses?" I asked.

"Sure, pink's a nice color. Here, go put these flowers back in the car."

I took the vase, trying not to look at his face, knowing that stifling a tear was even harder if he knew I was watching him. I sat in the car, the motor running, holding the vase of roses. Then I saw Levi take something from his coat pocket and tuck it down inside the stone vase. It appeared to be a piece of paper, though I couldn't be sure.

The snow had started to fall in earnest and Levi shuffled back to the car. "Gonna be a big snow this time, I think. Let's get going."

I knew that the one thing he wouldn't discuss was the one thing on his mind. How could the heavy snowfall not remind him of this day 57 years earlier? At 15, I hadn't yet experienced a broken heart, but sitting with my great-granddad, I was near enough to feel it.

The following year I got my driver's license. It was my first time to drive to the family cemetery by myself. There was no snow this Valentine's Day, just a gray, dull chill.

The rose bush Levi and I had planted in April had bloomed beautifully through the summer. It looked rather somber now, as did the entire cemetery. The date of Levi's death had been carved on his stone four months earlier.

My parents had placed some silk poinsettias on the

grave at Christmas, and they were still there. Out of season now, I thought.

As I pulled them from the stone vase, something caught my eye. Barely visible in the pebbles at the bottom of the vase, I saw a corner of white paper. Somehow, after a year of snow and rain and wind, Levi's last paper snowflake was still intact.

I reached for it, thinking I would put it with my greatgrandparents' other belongings in my parents' basement.

But the paper wasn't a souvenir for me. It was Levi's anniversary gift. It needed to stay exactly where it was.

May you rejoice in the wife of your youth...
May you ever be captivated by her love.

KING SOLOMON

Spirit of Sunshine

AUTHOR UNKNOWN

"How's business, Eben?"

The old man was washing at the sink after his day's work.

"Fine, Marthy, fine."

"Does the store look just the same? Land, how I'd like to be there again with the sun shining in so bright! How does it look, Eben?"

"The store's never been the same since you left it, Marthy." A faint flush came into Martha's cheeks. Is a wife ever too old to be moved by her husband's praise?

For years Eben and Martha had kept a tiny notion store, but one day Martha fell sick and was taken to the hospital. That was months ago. She was out now, but she would never be strong again—never more be partner in the happy little store.

I can't help hankering for a sight of the store, thought Martha one afternoon. If I take it real careful I think I can get down there. 'Tisn't so far.

It took a long time for her to drag herself downtown, but at last she stood at the head of the little street where the store was. All of a sudden she stopped. Not far from her on the pavement stood Eben. A tray hung from his neck. On this tray were arranged a few cards of collar-buttons, some papers of pins and several bundles of shoelaces. In a trembling voice he called his wares.

Martha leaned for support against the wall of a building nearby. She looked over the way at the little store. Its windows were filled with fruit. Then she understood. The store had gone to pay her hospital expenses. She turned and hurried away as fast as her weak limbs would carry her.

It will hurt him so to have me find it out! she thought, and the tears trickled down her face.

He's kept it a secret from me, and now I'll keep it a secret from him. He shan't ever know that I know.

That night when Eben came in, chilled and weary, Martha asked cheerily the old question:

"How's business, Eben?"

"Better'n ever, Marthy," was the cheery answer, and Martha prayed God might bless him for his sunshiny spirit and love of her.

*Two persons must believe in each other,
and feel that it can be done and must be done;
in that way they are enormously strong.*

VINCENT VAN GOGH

Constancy

FRANK L. STANTON

It is something sweet when the world goes ill,
To know you are faithful and love me still;
To feel when the sunshine has left the skies,
That the light is shining in your dear eyes;
Beautiful eyes, more dear to me
Than all the wealth of the world could be.

It is something, dearest, to feel you near,
When life with its sorrows seems hard to bear;
To feel, when I falter, the clasp divine
Of your tender and trusting hand in mine;
Beautiful hand, more dear to me
Than the tenderest thing on earth could be.

Sometimes, dearest, the world goes wrong,

For God gives grief with His gift of song.

And poverty, too, but your love is more

To me than riches and golden store;

Beautiful love, until death shall part,

It is mine—as you are—my own sweetheart!

Ben and Virginia

GWYN WILLIAMS

*I*n 1904, a railroad camp of civil engineers was set up near Knoxville, Tennessee. The L & N campsite had tents for the men, a warm campfire, a good cook and the most modern surveying equipment available. In fact, working as a young civil engineer for the railroad at the turn of the century presented only one real drawback: a severe shortage of eligible young women.

Benjamin Murrell was one such engineer. A tall, reticent man with a quiet sense of humor and a great sensitivity for people, Ben enjoyed the nomadic railroad life. His mother had died when he was only thirteen, and this early loss caused him to become a loner.

Like all the other men, Ben sometimes longed for the companionship of a young woman, but he kept his thoughts between himself and God. On one particularly

memorable spring day, a marvelous piece of information was passed around the camp: The boss's sister-in-law was coming to visit! The men knew only three things about her: She was nineteen years old, she was single and she was pretty. By midafternoon the men could talk of little else. Her parents were sending her to escape the yellow fever that was invading the Deep South and she'd be there in only three days. Someone found a tintype of her, and the photograph was passed around with great seriousness and grunts of approval.

Ben watched the preoccupation of his friends with a smirk. He teased them for their silliness over a girl they'd never even met. "Just look at her, Ben. Take one look and then tell us you're not interested," one of the men retorted. But Ben only shook his head and walked away chuckling.

The next two days found it difficult for the men of the L & N engineering camp to concentrate. The train would be there early Saturday morning and they discussed their plan in great detail. Freshly bathed, twenty

heads of hair carefully greased and slicked back, they would all be there to meet that train and give the young woman a railroad welcome she wouldn't soon forget. She'd scan the crowd, choose the most handsome of the lot and have an instant beau. Let the best man win, they decided. And each was determined to be that man.

The men were too preoccupied to see Ben's face as he beheld the picture of Virginia Grace for the first time. They didn't notice the way he cradled the photograph in his big hands like a lost treasure, or that he gazed at it for a long, long time. They missed the expression on his face as he looked first at the features of the delicate beauty, then at the camp full of men he suddenly perceived to be his rivals. And they didn't see Ben go into his tent, pick up a backpack and leave camp as the sun glowed red and sank beyond a distant mountain.

Early the next morning, the men of the L & N railroad camp gathered at the train station. Virginia's family, who had come to pick her up, rolled their eyes and tried

unsuccessfully not to laugh. Faces were raw from unaccustomed shaves, and the combination of men's cheap colognes was almost obnoxious. Several of the men had even stopped to pick bouquets of wildflowers along the way.

At long last the whistle was heard and the eagerly awaited train pulled into the station. When the petite, vivacious little darling of the L & N camp stepped onto the platform, a collective sigh escaped her would-be suitors. She was even prettier than the tintype depicted. Then every man's heart sank in collective despair. For there, holding her arm in a proprietary manner and grinning from ear to ear, was Benjamin Murrell. And from the way she tilted her little head to smile up into his face, they knew their efforts were in vain.

"How," his friends demanded of Ben later, "did you do that?"

"Well," he said, "I knew I didn't have a chance with all you scoundrels around. I'd have to get to her first if I wanted her attention, so I walked down to the previous

station and met the train. I introduced myself as a member of the welcoming committee from her new home."

"But the nearest station is seventeen miles away!" someone blurted incredulously. "You walked seventeen miles to meet her train? That would take all night!"

"That it did," he affirmed.

Benjamin Murrell courted Virginia Grace, and in due time they were married. They raised five children and buried one, a twelve-year-old son. I don't think they tried to build the eternal romance that some women's magazines

claim is so important. Nor did they have a standing Friday night date. In fact, Ben was so far out in the sticks while working on one engineering job that one of their children was a full month old before he saw his new daughter. Ben didn't take Virginia to expensive restaurants, and the most romantic gift he ever brought her was an occasional jar of olives. If Virginia ever bought a fetching nightgown and chased him around the icebox, that secret remains buried with her to this day.

What I do know is that they worked together on their relationship by being faithful to one another, treating each other with consideration and respect, having a sense of humor, bringing up their children in the knowledge of love of the Lord, and loving one another through some very difficult circumstances.

I am one of Benjamin and Virginia's great-grandchildren. He died when I was a baby, unfortunately, so I have no memory of him. NaNa (Virginia) died when I was twelve and she was eighty-five. When I knew her she was a

shriveled old woman who needed assistance to get around with a walker and whose back was hunched over from osteoporosis. Her aching joints were swollen with arthritis and her eyesight was hindered by the onset of glaucoma. At times, though, those clouded eyes would sparkle and dance with the vivaciousness of the girl my great-grandfather knew. They danced especially when she told her favorite story. It was the story of how she was so pretty that once, on the basis of a tintype, an entire camp turned out to meet the train and vie for her attention. It was the story of how one man walked seventeen miles, all night long, for a chance to meet the woman of his dreams and claim her for his wife.

We attract hearts by qualities we display:
we retain them by the qualities we possess.

JEAN BAPTISTE SUARD

91

Long-Term Romance

RUTH BELL GRAHAM

Mother had had a stroke several years before which had left her confined to a wheelchair, with her speech slightly affected. Frequently Daddy was up at four in the morning to have his Bible study and time of prayer so he could devote the rest of his day to Mother.

I stood by to help in any way I could, often taking the evening meal to them and bringing Mother to stay with me when Daddy would have to be gone for several days.

One morning when I dropped by to see how they were, I found Daddy on his knees in front of Mother, helping her put on her stockings.

Daddy had reached the point where he got up and down with difficulty. He, who had been an athlete in his younger days, and had always kept himself in top physical shape, now found himself with a painfully ulcerated

toe that refused to heal due to the fact that he was a bor-derline diabetic and had lost circulation in his left leg.

He glanced up at me over his glasses, giving me his usual broad smile of welcome.

"You know," he said, returning to Mother's stocking, "these are the happiest days of our lives. Caring for your mother is the greatest privilege of my life."

And the nice thing was, he meant it.

*Love, like a lamp, needs to be fed out of the oil
of another's heart, or its flame burns low.*

HENRY WARD BEECHER

*What's the earth with all its art, verse, music worth—
compared with love, found, gained and kept.*

ROBERT BROWNING

The Gift of the Magi

O. HENRY

One dollar and eighty-seven cents. That was all. And sixty cents of it was in pennies. Pennies saved one and two at a time by bulldozing the grocer and the vegetable man and the butcher until one's cheeks burned with the silent imputation of parsimony that such close dealing implied. Three times Della counted it. One dollar and eighty-seven cents. And the next day would be Christmas.

There was clearly nothing to do but flop down on the shabby little couch and howl. So Della did. Which instigates the moral reflection that life is made of sobs, sniffles, and smiles, with sniffles predominating.

While the mistress of her home is gradually subsiding from the first stage to the second, take a look at the home. A furnished flat at $8 per week. It did not exactly

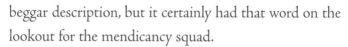

beggar description, but it certainly had that word on the lookout for the mendicancy squad.

In the vestibule below was a letter-box into which no letter would go, and an electric button from which no mortal finger could coax a ring. Also pertaining thereunto was a card bearing the name, "Mr. James Dillingham Young."

The "Dillingham" had been flung to the breeze during a former period of prosperity when its possessor was being paid $30 per week. Now, when the income was shrunk to $20, the letters of "Dillingham" looked blurred, as though they were thinking seriously of contracting to a modest and unassuming D. But whenever Mr. James Dillingham Young came home and reached his flat above he was called Jim and greatly hugged by Mrs. James Dillingham Young, already introduced to you as Della. Which is all very good.

Della finished her cry and attended to her cheeks with the powder rag. She stood by the window and looked out dully at a gray cat walking a gray fence in a gray backyard. Tomorrow would be Christmas Day, and she had only $1.87 with which to buy Jim a present. She had been saving every penny she could for months, with this result. Twenty dollars a week doesn't go far. Expenses had been greater than she had calculated. They always are. Only $1.87 to buy a present for Jim. Her Jim. Many a happy hour she had spent planning for something nice for him. Something fine and rare and sterling—something just a little bit near to being worthy of the honor of being owned by Jim.

There was a pier-glass between the windows of the room. Perhaps you have seen a pier-glass in an $8 flat. A very thin and very agile person may, by observing his reflection in a rapid sequence of longitudinal strips, obtain a fairly accurate conception of his looks. Della, being slender, had mastered the art.

Suddenly she whirled from the window and stood before the glass. Her eyes were shining brilliantly, but her

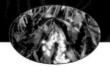

face had lost its color within twenty seconds. Rapidly she pulled down her hair and let it fall to its full length.

Now, there were two possessions of the James Dillingham Youngs in which they both took a mighty pride. One was Jim's gold watch that had been his father's and his grandfather's. The other was Della's hair. Had the Queen of Sheba lived in the flat across the airshaft, Della would have let her hair hang out the window some day to dry just to deprecate Her Majesty's jewels and gifts. Had King Solomon been the janitor, with all his treasures piled up in the basement, Jim would have pulled out his watch every time he passed, just to see him pluck at his beard from envy.

So now Della's beautiful hair fell around her rippling and shining like a cascade of brown waters. It reached below her knee and made itself almost a garment for her. And then she did it up again nervously and quickly. Once she faltered for a minute and stood still while a tear or two splashed on the worn red carpet.

On went her old brown jacket; on went her old brown hat. With a whirl of skirts and with the brilliant sparkle still in her eyes, she fluttered out the door and down the stairs to the street.

Where she stopped the sign read: "Mme. Sofronie. Hair Goods of All Kinds." One flight up Della ran, and collected herself, panting. Madame, large, too white, chilly, hardly looked the "Sofronie."

"Will you buy my hair?" asked Della.

"I buy hair," said Madame. "Take yer hat off and let's have a sight at the looks of it."

Down rippled the brown cascade.

"Twenty dollars," said Madame, lifting the mass with a practiced hand.

"Give it to me quick," said Della.

Oh, and the next two hours tripped by on rosy wings. Forget the hashed metaphor. She was ransacking the stores for Jim's present.

She found it at last. It surely had been made for Jim

and no one else. There was no other like it in any of the stores, and she had turned all of them inside out. It was a platinum fob chain simple and chaste in design, properly proclaiming its value by substance alone and not by meretricious ornamentation—as all good things should do. It was even worthy of The Watch. As soon as she saw it she knew that it must be Jim's. It was like him. Quietness and value—the description applied to both. Twenty-one dollars they took from her for it, and she hurried home with the 87 cents. With that chain on his watch Jim might be properly anxious about the time in any company. Grand as the watch was, he sometimes looked at it on the sly on account of the old leather strap that he used in place of a chain.

When Della reached home her intoxication gave way to prudence and reason. She got out her curling irons and lighted the gas and went to work repairing the ravages made by generosity added to love. Which is always a treacherous task, dear friends—a mammoth task.

Within forty minutes her head was covered with tiny, close-lying curls that made her look wonderfully like a truant schoolboy. She looked at her reflection in the mirror long, carefully, and critically.

"If Jim doesn't kill me," she said to herself, "before he takes a second look at me, he'll say I look like a Coney Island chorus girl. But what could I do—oh! what could I do with a dollar and eighty-seven cents?"

At 7 o'clock the coffee was made and the frying pan was on the back of the stove and was ready to cook the chops.

Jim was never late. Della doubled the fob chain in her hand and sat on the corner of the table near the door that he always entered. Then she heard his step on the stair away down on the first flight, and she turned white for just a moment. She had a habit of saying little silent prayers about the simplest everyday things, and now she whispered, "Please, God, make him think I am still pretty."

The door opened and Jim stepped in and closed it. He looked thin and very serious. Poor fellow, he was only

twenty-two—and to be burdened with a family! He needed a new overcoat and he was without gloves.

Jim stopped inside the door, as immovable as a setter at the scent of a quail. His eyes were fixed upon Della, and there was an expression in them that she could not read, and it terrified her. It was not anger, nor surprise, nor disapproval, nor horror, nor any of the sentiments that she had been prepared for. He simply stared at her fixedly with that peculiar expression on his face.

Della wriggled off the table and went for him.

"Jim, darling," she cried, "don't look at me that way. I had my hair cut off and sold it because I couldn't have lived through Christmas without giving you a present. It'll grow again—you won't mind, will you? I just had to do it. My hair grows awfully fast. Say 'Merry Christmas!' Jim, and let's be happy. You don't know what a nice— what a beautiful, nice gift I've got for you."

"You've cut your hair off?" asked Jim, laboriously, as if he had not arrived at that patent fact yet even after the hardest mental labor.

"Cut it off and sold it," said Della. "Don't you like me just as well, anyhow? I'm me without my hair, ain't I?"

Jim looked around the room curiously.

"You say your hair is gone?" he said, with an air almost of idiocy.

"You needn't look for it," said Della. "It's sold, I tell you—sold and gone, too. It's Christmas Eve, boy. Be good to me, for it went for you. Maybe the hairs of my head were numbered," she went on with a sudden serious sweetness, "but nobody could ever count my love for you. Shall I put the chops on, Jim?"

Out of his trance Jim seemed quickly to wake. He enfolded his Della. For ten seconds let us regard with discreet scrutiny some inconsequential object in the other direction. Eight dollars a week or a million a year—what is the difference? A mathematician or a wit would give you the wrong answer. The magi brought valuable gifts, but that was not among them. This dark assertion will be illuminated later on.

Jim drew a package from his overcoat pocket and threw it upon the table.

"Don't make any mistake, Dell," he said, "about me. I don't think there's anything in the way of a haircut or a shave or a shampoo that could make me like my girl any less. But if you'll unwrap that package you might see why you had me going a while at first."

White fingers and nimble tore at the string and paper.

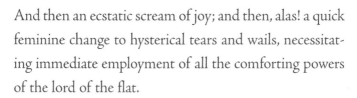

And then an ecstatic scream of joy; and then, alas! a quick feminine change to hysterical tears and wails, necessitating immediate employment of all the comforting powers of the lord of the flat.

For there lay The Combs—the set of combs, side and back, that Della had worshipped for long in a Broadway window. Beautiful combs, pure tortoise shell, with jeweled rims—just a shade to wear in the beautiful vanished hair. They were expensive combs, she knew, and her heart had simply craved and yearned over them without the least hope of possession. And now, they were hers, but

the tresses that should have adorned the coveted adornments were gone.

But she hugged them to her bosom, and at length she was able to look up with dim eyes and a smile and say: "My hair grows so fast, Jim!"

And then Della leaped up like a little singed cat and cried, "Oh, oh!"

Jim had not yet seen his beautiful present. She held it out to him eagerly upon her open palm. The dull precious metal seemed to flash with a reflection of her bright and ardent spirit.

"Isn't it a dandy, Jim? I hunted all over town to find it. You'll have to look at the time a hundred times a day now. Give me your watch. I want to see how it looks on it."

Instead of obeying, Jim tumbled down on the couch and put his hands under the back of his head and smiled.

"Dell," said he, "let's put our Christmas presents away and keep 'em a while. They're too nice to use just at present. I sold the watch to get the money to buy your combs.

And now suppose you put the chops on."

The magi, as you know, were wise men—wonderfully wise men—who brought gifts to the Babe in the manger. They invented the art of giving Christmas presents. Being wise, their gifts were no doubt wise ones, possibly bearing the privilege of exchange in case of duplication. And here I have lamely related to you the uneventful chronicle of two foolish children in a flat who most unwisely sacrificed for each other the greatest treasures of their house. But in a last word to the wise of these days let it be said that of all who give gifts these two were the wisest. Of all who give and receive gifts, such as they are wisest. Everywhere they are the wisest. They are the magi.

Love cannot stay at home; a man cannot keep it
to himself. Like light, it is constantly traveling.
A man must spend it, must give it away.

NORMAN MACLEOD

109

Titanic Love

JIM PRIEST

They were the picture of romance as they strolled the deck of the luxury ocean liner.

Arm in arm they walked, heads together, sharing stories and secrets and smiles.

From what people could see, they seemed very much in love. But beneath the surface, where no one could see, there was something else. Something that eyes could not behold, that ears could not hear and that minds could not grasp.

Beneath the surface was a deep and abiding commitment to one another that welded them together stronger and tighter than the rivets holding the unsinkable ship they were aboard.

Their names were Isidor and Ida Strauss.

Immigrants to America, they had scratched and scrapped their way in the new world and made a name for themselves.

With sweat and smarts, they had been able to build a little merchandise store in New York City: they named it Macy's. As they walked the decks of the HMS *Titanic* that April day in 1912, they were enjoying a much deserved vacation. They were enjoying each other's company. Unknown to them they were enjoying their last day together.

It was April 14, 1912, late in the evening, when the *Titanic*—the unsinkable ship crossing the Atlantic on her maiden voyage—struck an iceberg and started to sink. Icebergs, of course, only show a small part of themselves, most of the imponderable chunk of ice is below the ocean's surface.

Beneath the surface where no eye could see, no ear could hear, no mind could grasp its depth and size. As the ship began to list and take on water the lives of those on board began to change.

Some fearfully scrambled for safety. Some valiantly helped those in need. Isidor and Ida Strauss walked calmly on the deck, assessing the situation before finally approaching a lifeboat. Mrs. Strauss began to climb into the lifeboat, but changed her mind at the last minute.

She turned to her husband and said, "We have been living together for many years. Where you go, I go."

Members of the crew overheard her and tried to get her to change her mind. She would not listen.

A crew member turned to old Mr. Strauss and said, "I'm sure no one would object to an old gentleman like yourself getting in."

But Mr. Strauss was as stubborn as his wife.

"I will not go before the other men."

So the issue was settled. Neither would go without the other, and neither one would go.

Mrs. Strauss turned to her maid, now safely on board the lifeboat and said, "Here, take my fur coat. I won't be needing it."

Then the old couple walked a few steps to some nearby deck chairs and sat down together to await the inevitable.

Like the iceberg, the Strausses had more beneath the surface than could be seen by a casual observer. True enough, they showed their love for one another, but that was just the part that was visible. Beneath the surface was a solid commitment to one another that nothing, not even the threat of death could shake.

*Love comforteth
like sunshine
after rain.*

WILLIAM SHAKESPEARE

Life's Finest Hour

EUGENE S. GEISSLER

Do you remember, Jo, when you first called me "Friend Husband"? It was many, many years ago, early in our marriage. I don't think it struck me as particularly extraordinary at first to be called that name. After all, what else is expected from a husband or wife? But now that I am old and you still say it, it has grown into considerable significance for me.

We have been through a lot together and having survived it all. We look forward to continued care for each other. Our tenderness is more precious than ever because of our greater need for each other.

Thirty-five years into our marriage you wrote, "Friend Husband was 20 when I met him—so I have no first-hand knowledge of his early years. The person he was at 28 commanded my immediate interest—there was no strangeness, no tension—and we were friends from our first meeting. And we remain friends together."

Short days ago we quietly celebrated 45 years of marriage. It was indeed one of our finest anniversaries, wasn't it? The next day you took me aside though there was nobody around that could see or hear us. You confided: "Ever since we've been married and then when you were overseas, and all these years since, I've wanted to buy you a gold wedding band. Would you wear it?"

So I sit here with my golden wedding band shining at me. I've had it on less than 45 hours, but it fits and feels

like it has been there for 45 years. The next time I left a note for you on the kitchen counter, I delighted in signing it: "Friend Husband w/ the gold ring."

Am I just talking trivia? Or is it perhaps not necessary to say anything? A husband and a wife, friends together for 45 years, might just know what the other is thinking. At the end of such a long period of time, sitting silently together becomes a kind of virtue, a pleasing sound, a language of presence. Would you say that every now and then we are inclined to call it "life's finest hour"?

Five years ago our children decided to re-do our family room into a room for just the two of us. We were caught by surprise, not feeling secure about the offer. You know how people growing older don't like things being changed around. But it was a Christmas present, lovingly signed by our children.

It is a rather long but somewhat narrow room, facing south and front, with a large picture window. On the narrow east end of the room is the library. There you have the wing chair you have always wanted, and there you spend a lot of time reading. Reading is your pastime, much of your entertainment, your therapy and refuge.

My wing chair, matching yours across the room, sits in the corner next to the stove. It's my home base. A couch against the wall opposite the window allows for some good company now and then.

So here we are, daily facing each other across the room—you in the library most of the time, and myself, an up-and-down, in-and-out person, only half as much. But much happens between us here. We say prayers together; we often eat our breakfast and lunch here. We interrupt each other with things to tell, insights to offer, deep thoughts to share, jokes to laugh at, even disagreements to start and stop.

We are aware of our need for each other, our concern for each other, our promises to take care of each other, whichever one is able to do so when that time comes. Sometimes we ask the Lord if we might die close together.

Every day we thank God for our being together.

Among the people we seem to pray for more often now are "the old and the infirm," and the other morning we had to add: "among whom we class ourselves." Neither of us is either that old or that infirm to be talking much about it. Still we know it to be coming—the end of those things we have cherished together. To be honest about what lies hidden before us doesn't distract us from those fleeting moments of peace and quiet of soul, which are a foretaste of the good things that wait us in the presence of the Lord.

In all our losses, all our gains,
In all our pleasures, all our pains,
The life of life is: Love remains.
In every change from good to ill,
If love continue still,
Let happen then what will.

THEODORE TILTON

We Have Lived and Loved Together

CHARLES JEFFREYS

We have lived and loved together
Through many changing years;
We have shared each other's gladness
And wept each other's tears;
I have known ne'er a sorrow
That was long unsoothed by thee;
For thy smiles can make a summer
Where darkness else would be.

Like the leaves that fall around us
In autumn's fading hours,
Are the traitor's smiles that darken
When the cloud of sorrow lowers,
And though many such we've known, love,
Too prone, alas, to range,
We both can speak of one love
Which time can never change.

We have lived and loved together
Through many changing years,
We have shared each other's gladness
And wept each other's tears.

And let us hope the future,
As the past has been will be:
I will share with thee my sorrows,
And thou thy joy with me.

Acknowledgments

A diligent search has been made to trace original ownership, and when necessary, permission to reprint has been obtained. If I have overlooked giving proper credit to anyone, please accept my apologies. Should any attribution be found to be incorrect, the publisher welcomes written documentation supporting correction for subsequent printings. For material not in the public domain, grateful acknowledgment is given to the publishers and individuals who have granted permission for use of their material.

Acknowledgments are listed by story title in the order they appear in the book. For permission to reprint any of the stories, please request permission from the original source listed below.

"A Gentle Caress" by Daphna Renan. Used by permission of the author. Daphna Renan has published several short stories in several anthologies. She can be contacted by e-mail at daphna.renan@yale.edu.

"Do You Remember Me?" by Arnold Fine, the senior editor of The Jewish Press. Used by permission of the author.

"The Mystery of Marriage" by Mike Mason from *The Mystery of Marriage* (Multnomah Publishers, Inc., Sisters, Oregon) © 1985. Used by permission of the author.

"Love in a Locket" by Geery Howe, M.A., a consultant, international speaker, and trainer in leadership, management, and strategic change and development. Author of *Listen to the Heart*. Check out his website at http://www.members.aol.com/geeryhowe/.

"With This Ring" by Ruth Bell Graham taken from *Ruth Bell Graham's Collected Poems* © 1995, published by Baker Book House Company.

"House on the Lake" by Mike Royko. Reprinted with special permission from the *Chicago Sun-Times, Inc.* © 2001 and with permission from the December 1997 *Reader's Digest*.

"Levi's Valentine" by J. Stephen Lang © 2000. Used by permission of the author.